TRACY BIHARY

Chocolate Cake In Heaven

A journey through the act of abortion to

Finding forgiveness from the Lord

All proceeds from the sale of this book will be sent to the
Cleveland Pregnancy Center for their continued support
and help towards saving the lives of the unborn.
Please visit www.chocolatecakeinheaven.com

ISBN: 1-4563-2927-8
ISBN-13: 9781456329273

DEDICATION

For my children:
Savannah Grace, David Caleb, Nathanial John,
Brittany Danielle, Antony Lee,
Christopher Alan and Gwenyth Georgia.
May you know the Lord with all His heart and love.
May we never be apart.

Thank you Brittany for the Chocolate Cake illustration!

Contents

Introduction

Matthew 18:10, 14 (Jesus said) "See that you do not look down on one of these little ones. For I tell you that their angels in heaven always see the face of my father in heaven....Your father in heaven is not willing that any of these little ones should be lost."

To write a story, it is often best to let the reader know some background information which casts the setting. This tale is set a little differently than a usual story book as clips of memories are laid out for you to read; rather than typical chapters. This is a running account of a dark and bleak time set ten years ago. I had already been through a divorce from a ten year marriage with a forming alcoholic and, through another relationship been a survivor of domestic violence where I was mentally, physically and sexually abused; even raped, yet my next relationship took me on a path of helplessness, utter despair and self destruction. The reader must know that whilst the alcoholism and abuse are only mentioned here, it by no means lessens the terrible impact they individually held upon my soul. This book is therefore for another tragedy that befell my life but one that I was entirely responsible for.

Let me take you on a journey; walk with me for just a while and go the distance of self loathing and hatred to finding forgiveness and love from the Lord. Witness a firsthand account to the sad reality of abortion; the truth behind the 'quick fix' and the path forward to receiving inner peace. Even one life saved is one life to be lived; a life that can bring love, laughter and joy into the world. Walk in my shoes for just a moment so that you too can hopefully help save a life that is so precious to the Lord and help end the terrible disease of abortion that prevails in this world.

We don't know ahead of time the journey of life; where it will take us and what lessons we will learn along the way. Life is a constant school and every day brings messages, trials, tribulations and accomplishments to us all.

As an only child, I was very much loved by my parents and felt very close to both my mother and father; always wrapped around my mother's leg and the apple of my father's eye. Yet one constant fear I remember throughout my childhood was the understanding that one day I would die; that one day my mother and father would pass away and that I'd never physically see them again. I often thought deeply of the physical aspects of death; not breathing and not existing which terrified me greatly. I believed in God but had so many questions that I thought perhaps I was not Godly or Christian enough to go to heaven. Ironically, by the time I was twenty, death and I became well acquainted as I'd been to so many funerals that I'd lost count of them. Death was always there, hanging over me like a distant shadow. So many people, so many close relatives had gone. Consequently, life was something I held very precious in my hand that could not be taken lightly.

As I prepared to research and write this personal account of abortion, I searched out the abortion clinic that I went to on that fateful day. I remembered so much about the building and the moments within the cold and indifferent surrounding walls yet I could not remember the exact location of where I had gone. It had been ten long years, but when the on-line search engine found abortion clinics within the vicinity, it showed one with the exact photo images of the building that I had held scorched in my memory for all that time. Even though I have gone through the darkness and have found forgiveness, memories are sometimes hard to face especially when you can see actual pictures of a place that holds such horror. Yet, I know that the Lord is with me as I write and move forward; I have a job to do, similar to a reporter who tells a story of an event or incident so that it can reach the masses and inform them enough to make a different decision to what might have previously been made.

I was raised a Christian but only dabbled in my faith from time to time, however, my personal relationship with God began at an early age. I was five years old when my mother asked me who my friends were at school and whom I played with at recess. I replied that God was my friend and that He and I had spoken through many lunch breaks. I would occasionally wonder off by myself and sit under the apple tree at the far end of the playing field on the school grounds; perhaps as an only child I was comfortable with being alone, as I always had God with me, that is until the teenage years came along and swept me up and away with the local 'in crowd' who didn't want to be part of the God Squad as they called it; then the questions started to formulate. I wanted to know the Truth and know definitely without a shadow of a doubt that Darwin was wrong and the Lord was real. I think many of us question God's existence but through my own investigation and evidence I thankfully know Him to be true.

God and I had a hide and seek relationship in my youth; one I would describe as the Lord frequently going fishing for me. He would cast out His fishing line, pull me in and I would bask in His love, just for a while until I came back to earth with a thud where everyday life, trouble and turmoil took over in lead position. He would seek me out when I least expected it and I loved being part of Him, but every surrounding sight and sound around me would steal me away and I would forget who was in charge and take over myself, making my own decisions and not letting Him decide what direction I should take. Anyone can come to the Lord, but you often find yourself brought before Him when you are in the midst and deepest depths of tragedy. The Lord is wondrous in how He works; He can lead the way and be the truth and the light.

He finally caught this fish ten years ago; ten long years of a story, testimony and prayer waiting to be told.

Psalm 139:13-16 "God, you created my inmost being; you knit me together in my mother's womb....All the days ordained for me were written in your book before one of them came to be."

ৡৈ৶ঌ

Savannah's Message

Momma, I can see you as I sit against His feet,
You know that one day we will hug upon our chance to meet.
And you will see the lives we save; our story's not in vain,
To reach out; stop the killing, end the needless death and pain.
I've waited for this moment momma; know that I love you,
And that I'm with you every day in everything you do.

Read this book and story please to share with whom
you know,
Let momma's words reach out to you to plant a seed
and grow.
Heaven's much too crowded now with babies just like me,
Please help end all abortions, help the government to see.

........*Savannah Grace—voice of the unborn, yet alive with
Jesus!*
ॐॐ

PART I
THE DARKNESS

Chapter 1
The Abortion Clinic

Isaiah 64:8 "Yet, O Lord, you are our Father. We are the clay, you are the potter; we are all the work of your hand."

I could hear the hardened ice crunching against the grey snow underneath my boyfriend's shabby work boots; one foot at a time, slowly grinding each step whilst he held my arm to steady my balance. I felt so stupid; slipping on a sheet of clear ice outside the backdoor of the apartment building on my way to work a few days earlier, hitting the ground with a thud and pulling multiple muscles in my back that I didn't know I had. The pain had been excruciating but as always, life went on and I managed to maneuver my sore body from one place to the next. How ironic to say life goes on!

As we approached the abortion clinic, I could hear the wind whistle and whip round the side of the gray stone building; I could see breath escape my mouth like a white fog, but, I couldn't feel the cold or ice piercing my heart. Not today.

Many angry protesters stood outside the depressing cold and stark building on that fateful Saturday in January, wrapped up in thick heavy coats and warm hats and gloves, waving their explicit placards and posters of aborted babies. I didn't even expect to see anyone outside; it didn't occur to me that this issue was one so many people were passionate about. I could hear shouts and pleading cries of pain and anguish but all was in vein as I moved forward with my head down and up the snow covered steps. It was the march of the condemned to the executioner's block, yet the cries were of pure innocence; not guilty, not yet. Guilt would indeed find and seek me out taking its own heavy toll of punishment. The grim reaper only had eyes on my baby today and of course my soul. I'd paid the executioner a sum of $300 which was the amount of what a human life was worth there.

The waiting room was full; just like any other medical waiting room, maxed to the brim of patients waiting to see their doctors, yet this waiting room was masked in an extraordinary fashion and not for those with colds and minor injuries. Doctors' waiting rooms were usually quiet with the odd conversation taking place, the rustling pages of magazines turning, an occasional child talking or several children playing with a box of toys. Yet this waiting room was a far cry from that normality and almost snarled at me with evil reverence. The noise level was at a maximum; women laughed with exuberance, conversations could be heard by everyone and in fact, everyone could join in the same conversation, it didn't matter. A few men who were scattered around the room socialized at a more somber level and, there were no children...so to speak...their voices unheard and they remained unseen.

"I'm here for a 10:00 o'clock appointment" I said nervously to the woman who sat behind the glass reception window.

4

"Name?" she asked. I looked nervously at her and whispered so as not to reveal who I was. Did I really think someone in that room would know me? Did it matter?

"Take a seat" she replied without looking up; whipping her pencil at the direction of where I was to sit. I noticed the grey hairs mixed with dark black on top of her head and wondered at her age; forty or perhaps fifty? How long had she been at this job; seeing thousands of women walk in and out every day, walking in whole and walking out in fragmented pieces. As we looked for a couple of empty chairs, a young couple beckoned from the other side of the room. "There's no seats left in there, we had to come out into the hallway" said the man; was he the husband, fiancé or boyfriend I wondered? Again, it didn't matter.

As we sat rather uncomfortably on the staircase, the shabby work boots stared at me whilst my boyfriend, the father of the baby I was about to abort, began talking to the friendly couple. I could hear a conversation taking place with the woman laughing; voices were muffled and resonated unclearly in my head as if I were drugged or perhaps just waking up from a deep sleep, yet I was neither. I noticed a door at the other end of the waiting room that patients disappeared through when their names were called, never to return. Was this a gas chamber in a Nazi concentration camp; perhaps we were to line up, strip naked to the bone and prepare for death? No, but the thousands of babies that came into that building were. The clock ticked by slowly; time slipping through the executioners hands. The room began to empty, couple by couple and one by one and even though every ounce of me knew I should not have been in that room, I stayed, praying to get it all over with so that life

5

could go on. When seats became available, we followed our new acquaintances to some empty chairs within the main waiting area and sat down. I felt no difference between the hard staircase and the blue foam chair that I now sat on; I felt nothing at all. I knew that my back was throbbing as if an electric drill was coursing its way into my flesh, but still, I felt nothing. Numbness often seems to counteract pain. Perhaps it is nature's way of hiding from the truth.

I looked around the room with its white painted walls; obviously the clinic was in a dress up costume; this was Halloween and the clinic was pretending to be an ortho-dox medical facility. The large oversized clock stared back at me with deafening seconds ticking by. I wondered if the contractors who had painted the facility had known they were painting a house of death. Could the clock smith have known that the second hand on that specific clock would be the count down to thousands of innocent lives lost? Tic… toc…tic…toc…tic…toc. I felt as if I was losing my mind yet still I sat going through the motions like a machine.

Why couldn't they hurry up! Why couldn't this be over with! The quicker that I could be seen, the easier it would be to believe I'd never been there. I could pretend that it had never happened and my life would go back to normal. I looked around and wondered how I had even got here!

Life often throws moments that are seemingly sur-real and this was *my* ultimate surreal moment that would reign supreme for the rest of my life. Surreal; such a strange word. Something real that isn't. I was in the waiting room of impending doom, about to kill a human being. How could *I* have been there? *Me!*

Chapter 2
Mr. P.

Deuteronomy 30:19 "This day I call heaven and earth as witnesses against you that I have set before you life and death, blessings and curses. Now choose life, so that you and your children may live..."

I was the friend of friends growing up in London. During my school years, the old rotary style telephone and I were constant companions as I sat through hours and hours of girlfriend problems and issues. I was the ear that people borrowed and the shoulder that friends leant on. If ever there was someone who could be counted on, it was me; so why was I here?

I was the child that couldn't watch cruelty to animals on television; that wanted to become a vegetarian and who would avoid stepping on insects as life was to be respected in all realms, no matter what creature; so why was I here?

I was the young adult who once saved a pigeon that lay wounded at the side of the road. I'd been on my way home when I saw a bird laying helpless, wings astray and crippled. I'd stopped the car, got out and bent down to see the bird in terrible pain, trying to move its broken wing. Carefully I picked the bird up, gently laid it down on the front seat and drove slowly to the nearest veterinary clinic where I named it Mr. P. I called the veterinary surgery every day for two weeks, anxiously checking up on the bird's health until

Tracy Bihary

Mr. P. was completely healed and the vet let him fly away to his new found freedom. I paid almost $300 for Mr. P. to be mended and put back together, so how was it possible that I was in a waiting room in an abortion clinic, spending $300 to kill my own baby! But, I wasn't thinking about Mr. P. at that moment; he was the farthest thing from my mind as was God. I was thinking abstract thoughts to cover the erratic emotions running through my body. I was living in the moment with no concept or concern for the next five minutes, let alone the rest of my life. How strange that such a random act of kindness toward an innocent creature, years ago, would be such a prevalent image and memory in years to come. So why was I here?

Chapter 3
The Abortion Clinic

Deuteronomy 27:35 "Cursed is the man who accepts a bribe to kill an innocent person."

The nurse called my name. Should I even reference her as a nurse? To my notion, nurses are supposed to heal the sick and care for the wounded, not aid and abet in the death of an innocent baby! I left my boyfriend sitting in the waiting room, still talking to his new friends. He was the main perpetrator of why I was there in the first place. He didn't want this baby; his own flesh and blood and I, so weak by listening to everyone else's opinion and not my own heart, went along with the plan to quickly get rid of the problem.

I can only remember scattered pieces of the next hour; a snapshot of a room, a brief introductory conversation with some sort of counselor and questions that I could no more think clearly about than fly to the moon such as 'was I ready?' and 'had I thought everything through?'.

Memories are quite a unique concept as we can bury them so deep within us that we cannot fish them out again; but why would I ever want to remember this day? I would make this day non-existent in my memories; I'd wipe it from my mind and never think of it again. Oh, what foolish creatures we are that we live blinded by inaccurate truths for this memory is with me always. When the morning sun rises and I open my eyes I remember and think of the baby that I killed, yet the journey of self loathing to ultimate forgiveness is one I want to share.

I mumbled a response to the counselor's questions.

'Just go ahead and do this please'.

Being only five weeks pregnant was early in a first trimester and the counselor told me that it may have been too early for them to find the fetus. God no! I needed this done today! Now! I can't wait another week or so! This must happen now! Everyone has told me so! That I can't keep this baby! It must be gone…..now! I can't go through this again; being caught in an eternal loop, watching that stupid lady; me, go into the building over and over; reliving the nightmare that I had so easily fallen into. But this would be the best solution; the quick fix to the problem, then it would all go away.

Chapter 4
Mom

Psalm 139:13-16 "for you created my inmost being; you knit me together in my mother's womb. I praise you because I am fearfully and wonderfully made; your works are wonderful, I know that full well. My frame was not hidden from you when I was made in the secret place. When I was woven together in the depths of the earth, your eyes saw my unformed body. All the days ordained for me were written in your book before one of them came to be."

The previous week I'd called home.

"Mom, um, I'm pregnant", I whispered into the phone; whispered as I didn't want her to hear me or was it that I didn't want to hear the words out loud? I can only imagine the horror, fear and despair that she felt in one moment; her daughter, living so far away pregnant and divorced with two children.

"What! Well, you can't keep it!" she replied flustered and angry. "How stupid can you get, you've already got two children and certainly can't afford another. You are by yourself and can't do it!"

Her voice trailed off into the distance. My mother; a truly wonderful woman whom I'd admired and put on a pedestal all my life, a woman who was neither afraid of man nor beast, a fearless business woman with a heart of gold, a woman who would give the shirt of her back to anyone....

yet, a woman who was telling me to kill my child. But I knew deep down this would be her reaction; a mother terrified for her own child's mental and physical survival, alone in a foreign country and that is where within my mother's mind the thought process stopped. The children I already had she knew; the baby wasn't a baby, wasn't born and therefore didn't exist.

I loved my mother and father with all my heart; still do, and in my own mind, absolutely had to have my mother's blessing in everything I did, even if it meant trying to manipulate her to my way of thinking, but this was not a subject up for discussion.

'Your two children that you are already trying to raise alone have enough to worry about and need you. You will not be able to afford to clothe, feed and support another baby. What about day care and paying the rent and goodness only knows about the other bills and food! You just can't have this baby!'

The record of her frantic voice played over and over in my head and now the score lay two against one; the odds were beginning to stack against the baby. I often wonder where my voice was in all of this discussion; did I even have a strong opinion? I believe that being persuaded in a common direction is easy when you are lost as it provides a quick and simple solution to a problem.

One of the affects to come after the abortion was the devastating pull and separation from the close bond I had with my mother. The destruction of my baby almost destroyed my relationship with the one person that I idolized. As the days and weeks moved forward I began to harbor an inner anger and longing for my mother to realize what I had done was wrong. I needed her to see and admit as I did that abortion was not the answer and that her sweeping it under the carpet attitude, where it could be forgotten was the opposite of what should be done. I can't remember a more desperate longing for my mother than at that time. I had been so wonderfully blessed with such loving parents and the parody was the ultimate sin anyone could carry out.

Chapter 5
Nathaniel John and David Caleb

Isaiah 65:17, 19, 20 (God said) "Behold, I will create new heavens and a new earth. The former things will not be remembered nor will they come to mind...the sound of weeping and crying will be heard in it no more. Never again will there be in it an infant who lives but a few days..."

This book would not be complete without the addition of Nathanial and David; my two boys whom I'd miscarried whilst three months and six weeks pregnant respectfully. I had decided they were boys after my counseling, but I'm skipping ahead of the story. The loss of a child is the most devastating experience I believe that anyone can have. Lives are lost on a daily basis; fathers, mothers, sisters, brothers, other relatives and friends, and that is the circle of life that we are expected to follow; but to lose a child is not in the normal order of things. I believe one has to identify at what point life starts and ends to understand any concept within this book. To some, losing a child you don't even know cannot be something to regret or feel loss for, but to those that truly know the Lord; you will know that location is immaterial and that a life is a life from the moment of conception inside the womb until the day we die.

Tracy Bihary

I'd lost two boys at different times in my life; babies I had not seen or physically known, yet they are my babies who were lifted to glory, waiting for me to come home. The hardest notion to recognize is the abundant grief I felt from the loss of the two children that I had no hand in losing; the fact that I had already been down a road of loss, grief and sadness was inexcusable as seemingly I had not learned a thing. I moved from accepting Gods plan of needing my two babies to be with Him, to me, taking my own hand at giving Him back a child I decided that *I* didn't want? How arrogant was I?

At the age of twenty and from a holiday romance I fell pregnant with Nathaniel John. The pregnancy terminated on its own after three months. I hadn't told my mother or father for fear of what they would say and I could only imagine what other family and friends would have said about the situation. Oh how worried I was about other people and what they thought! The blood loss I endured was quite substantive and I remember being very afraid and not telling anyone, other than a friend of mine at the time who also happened to be pregnant. She terminated her baby at four months gestation. I often wonder how she is today and if she has come to know the Lord and perhaps found forgiveness.

At the age of twenty-eight, my husband at the time, and I had been married for five years and had two children Brittany and Antony. We had wanted one more child and I found myself pregnant again with David Caleb. I remember being so happy. At three months, I had an ultrasound as was the normal timing of obstetrician care to see the progression of the baby. As I lay on the hospital bed with a bladder about to burst from drinking ounces and ounces of water, I looked at the nurse and read the expression of concern on

16

her face. Her deep frown and puzzled look was enough for me to know that something was wrong. She left the room in quite a panic and I craned my neck around to the hospital monitor in the hope to see what the commotion was about; I can only describe what I saw as a blob of tissue. Instead of seeing a little baby laying securely within my body, growing slowly every day and forming into a beautiful little child, I saw the unformed pieces of a tiny frame that all combined together into a mass of tissue. The nurse returned with the doctor on call who told me that David Caleb had passed away what would appear to have been an entire six weeks earlier. I'd carried a dead baby around for six weeks and didn't know it. I felt deceived and tricked into loving a baby I didn't have. A cruel joke had been played on me and all the dreams of a life ahead instantly faded away. I was told that I needed surgery to have David taken away; my dead baby removed from my womb. I was angry and yet covered up my loss with a hardy spirit and jovial attitude. How could it be that years later I would have a living being removed from its safety and security and destroyed by my own hand? Is that satire or a paradox of inhumanity? After the surgery the doctor came to see me on his rounds. I greeted him with a full smile and positive attitude; making light of a situation was a diversion and meant I didn't have to deal with the situation at hand but he saw through the bravado; a way I often covered up fear and sadness.

"You need time to grieve" He said with kindness. Oh how those words he spoke would take on so much more meaning that he could possibly ever know.

Chapter 6
The Abortion Clinic

Exodus 20:1, 13 "And God spoke all these words:..."You shall not murder."

I don't remember walking into the room. I don't remember lying on the table. I don't remember having an anesthetic, but I do remember the doctor fumbling around with the ultrasound equipment and saying "I can't find it!" Utter panic attacked my mind! No, no, no!!!! You must find it, it's there! I know it is!

I wonder now how something so precious as a little baby be an 'it'.

The room was dark and dismal. I saw masked men at the foot of the table; was he like the masked men of years ago who executed prisoners. Masking provided executioners anonymity from expression of pity or even joy at the brutal work they carried out; was this reason the same for the masked doctors I saw? To the left of the wall medical devices and machines made low humming sounds and a nurse in a white uniform stood at my side. My heart was racing and my breathing erratic. "Can you see it?" I anxiously asked, hoping with every conscious thought that I possessed that the answer would be yes.

"There it is" came the reply that sounded one of relief as I fell into the oblivion of hell's restless sleep whilst the silent vacuum began its dutiful job of extracting my baby.

Tracy Bihary

I woke up in a type of recovery room to the sound of soft crying. A girl, much younger than me was to my left in a chair, sobbing uncontrollably as tears ran down her face. The crying seemed so empty, as if her soul had left and all that remained was a shell. I took her hand.

"What's the matter?" said the loud stern voice of the nurse who had returned into the room. "That's what you came in for wasn't it!"

I think at that moment the reality of what I had done swallowed me whole. I'd killed my baby! I later learned that many women don't feel the regret of their abortion until years later; but for me, the realization was instant. An hour ago, I'd been pregnant with a baby, a little human being that had a mommy; yet now I was empty of not only my baby but my soul too. The realization was as I can only describe like a thousand pieces of ice shards stabbing my entire body. My breath left my body as I gasped in shock at what I had done. "No, no, I want my baby back" were the cries of utter anguish that I heard resounding in my head. I was screaming but no sound was coming out. Panic shook my body and jolted me for a while into the harsh reality of my ungodly deed until I slowly found myself back in the groggy anesthetic stupor that coveted and masked my sin for just a little while longer.

Chapter 7
Home

Matthew 5:21 "You have heard that it was said to the people long ago, 'Do not murder, and anyone who murders will be subject to judgment."

I don't remember leaving the clinic or even the car ride home. I just remember the sofa and pillows that welcomed me to sleep and rest. I lay down whilst my boyfriend left the house; and disappeared running errands or whatever important things he thought he had to accomplish that day. Perhaps that was his way of not facing reality, I don't know.

Sounds of Pavarotti and the Three Tenors emanated from the television. I slept, drifting out of a drugged daze; not wanting to wake up and face the cold harsh reality of what was left of the day. The melodious opera sounds were comforting and for a while I was peaceful. Sleep can often be a friend and an escape from life and the pain it hides.

I slept for hours, waiting until I needed to go and collect the children from their friends house, and for just a short time more, I cast out any recollection of what I had done and where I had been that day.

Chapter 8
Monday

Exodus 23:7 "Have nothing to do with a false charge and do not put an innocent or honest person to death, for I will not acquit the guilty."

I hadn't ever given much thought to irony. It is a word that implies a sort of discrepancy between what is said or done and what is literally meant, yet what was about to happen was the most ironic moment I could ever imagine happening to anyone. By 8:00 am the next day, I dropped the children off at school and was on my way to work; life was a blur and I was struggling to comprehend what I had done and who I even was. The radio played in the background as I tried to focus on upcoming meetings, my micromanaging boss and numerous expense reports that I would need to file. But at that very moment, as I drove across the bridge on I480 East, I saw the most horrific sight I could ever have contemplated seeing. What was this! Was this my comeuppance! Was this the finger of God pointing at me! Was this the biggest joke that God could ever have the nerve to play!

Looming up on my right was a large bill board that showed a six foot fetus inside a womb staring at me! It was an opaque baby and I could see blood vessels, an eye and the water sac the child lived in. What was going on? My head swam! My stomach sunk and pitted inside out. Nausea rose up in the back of my throat and a sweeping panic engulfed my entire body. My heart began to race and at the same time broke into a million tiny fragmented pieces. Oh what irony to have had my abortion on a weekend that I knew nothing about; a weekend of the world trying to save the thousands of babies from their doom, a weekend meant to try and save the world. I felt the devils presence all around me as I read the big letters at the top of the billboard; Sanctity for Life and Right to Life Weekend!

I don't remember the remainder of the drive into work. I could not fathom how this was all happening and how I had found myself in an alternate life where I was now cast as a murderer. The girl who was so afraid of death had taken the life of her own child. I look back now and wonder how I survived even getting out of bed in the mornings as the guilt began weighing its heavy toll and I became so very desperate. Every morning I saw the billboard of the large fetus and by the time I got to work, I was a complete nervous and hysterical mess. I felt my soul tear into shreds and wondered how I could ever live my life whole and complete again. Taking care of two children and working as a single mother became a function of the new robot extension of me. I just lived with an empty heart and empty soul; the days, even years that followed, were the darkest I have known.

Chapter 9
Brittany and Antony
The Picture

Psalm 100:3 "Know that the Lord is God. It is He who made us, and we are his; we are his people, the sheep of his pasture."

The children and I had enjoyed Christmas and the holidays just a few brief weeks earlier. An abundance of presents was something I endeavored to achieve, even as a single parent. It was such a special time of the year laden with traditions that I tried to carry over from England to America; such as a turkey Christmas lunch with Christmas crackers and gifts left to open the next morning on Boxing Day. Life had been so much simpler even those few weeks prior and I longed for that time in my life again.

My daughter and I often enjoyed spending time in thrift stores, musing over the cast offs that other people discarded and finding new uses for items and clothing. Brittany my daughter was ten at the time of the abortion and my son Antony seven. They were extremely different in personalities; adding to that the diagnosis of Attention Deficit Hyperactivity Disorder with Antony at age five which is a challenging disorder to say the least. Brittany had been such a big help with her brother and often took a back seat for the amount of attention that Antony demanded. Her fire cracker personality blazed with fun, laughter and life and she would light up a room from her smile, yet her sensitive side was always in the forefront ready to detect hurt or sadness in others. Antony was a sensitive and loving son who looked up to his big sister for playful companionship and a second type of mothering that she gave him.

The thrift shop in the town was a frequent haunt of ours. Brittany loved the soft toys that were thread bear and needed love. She would feel sorry for them and want to give them a home; showering them her utmost attention and care. On one occasion we actually stopped along the side of the freeway to cut down a teddy bear that was left hanging on a sign post; the bear was soaked through with rain and muddy but he came home with us and still resides in our wicker basket of special cuddly toys. We are alike in so many ways. If there is a three and four legged dog needing a home, the three legged dog would take preference. We take the unwanted and rejected things in life and find them homes, places to live and people to love them.

I had given Brittany and Antony some money to spend in the thrift shop one particular Saturday and we spent our usual time just browsing through the crafts, books and toys that lay in abundance on the plentiful shelves. I remember the sun shining that day, even though the air was cold and sharp; hats, gloves and scarves were still an item of essential wear in January, and especially in Cleveland. We spent an hour or so looking around before I told her that we would need to get ready to leave.

"I won't be a minute" she said smiling. I want to buy something.

"Okay honey" I replied. Being ten, Brittany liked to be able to pay for things on her own and didn't want my help, so Antony and I walked over to the front window to see what was on display and let her enjoy being a grown up for a while. I was so proud of her and her heart of giving; little did I know she was about to give me the greatest message that I could ever have received.

We returned home and I parked as usual in the car lot to the large story apartment block that we had lived in for just over two years. I had been thinking of renting a house within the same locality; carting groceries up elevators and stairs with two young children was tiring and the thought of a driveway and ease of accessibility was extremely appealing. I busied myself with the evening chores, put the groceries away and was about to enter the bathroom to run the children's bath when Brittany stopped me in the hall way and said, "Here Mommy, I bought this for you today."

Being distracted when we left the thrift store, I had forgotten that she had bought something and hadn't realized at all that it would have been something for me.

"Thank you honey!" I expressed with a kiss. "What is it?"

She smiled as I opened up the flat parcel and looked down at one of the most wonderful gifts I have ever received. A pink wooden picture frame with a blue border held the background for a light brown teddy bear. He wore jean overalls and had a cute teddy face, but it wasn't the bear that caught my attention as much as the inscribed words written next to him.

"Children are a gift of the Lord….. Psalm 127-3."

I was in awe and amazement that this little girl would have bought me such a wonderful present and looking back, one that was a way of trying to give me a message from the Lord. His timing is truly impeccable as this was the week before I found out I was pregnant. I truly believe that He chose Brittany to talk to me; to try and make me see that what was about to happen would be a gift from Him and not a problem to destroy. I don't think that the Lord could have been any clearer in his wisdom of trying to send me a message of love, life and what it could bring; it was as clear as if He had picked up the telephone and said the words out loud.

Chapter 10
The Ballet Dancer

Hebrews 4:13 "Nothing in all creation is hidden from God's sight. Everything is uncovered and laid bare before the eyes of him to whom we must give account."

The days and weeks that followed the abortion were so dark and full of dread that I actually didn't exist as myself anymore. Trying to keep a job and function in the world of reality is so difficult when you are consumed by such a terror that it sweeps over you and actually takes your breath away. Anxiety and panic possessed my mind, body and soul from the minute I woke to the minute I actually fell asleep. I prayed for sleep to come quickly at night so that I would be able to forget for a while all the pain and guilt I felt; not suffer the stifling fear and not feel the torture that grappled with my mind every single waking minute of every day.

A few weeks passed and the weather was still bitterly cold. I parked the car as usual in the car lot at work and walked a short distance to the glass doors that held the warmth of the building inside. I was always in such a rush to get out of the cold but then one day on my way into the building, a ballet dancer appeared and the cold, icy wind didn't exist anymore; I was numb and everything was in slow motion.

The first time I saw her I was overjoyed and yet very afraid at the same time. A little girl of about five years of age was twirling in circles next to me dressed in a beautiful pink tutu and pink ballet shoes spinning around and around in a delicate pirouette. She was laughing and grasping for my hand. I stood still as the weather charred my face and battled with my coat; I was frozen in time.

I just knew it was my baby; a girl, and that she would have been a ballet dancer at that age. She was more of a picture in my mind than a hallucination, but an image that was very real and present. I was terrified that I was perhaps losing my mind! I couldn't understand what was happening to me and why I had such erratic thoughts and images thrust to the forefront of my imagination.

I continued to see the ballet dancer every morning yet as much of a comfort as this was, my heart broke into a million pieces of more guilt and torture; a constant reminder of the little baby I had killed, the little baby who would never be what my mind was showing me.

Every day the ballet dancer prodded my soul; she was with me from the moment I got out of the car until I entered the building at work and then she would leave me to face the day of terror ahead. I had been very lucky in my job to work for a company that had district managers who were always on the road and therefore I was left alone to open up the office and run the sales teams from the local hub. The solitude was my saving grace as I spent days upon weeks sobbing behind my desk, in the kitchen, the work room and large conference room. The crying was exhausting and the fatigue took over every ounce of spirit I had left. I longed for sleep; to switch off and leave the guilt for the next day. Switching gears when someone came in the office was one of the hardest accomplishments to make. The crying was obvious; blotchy, red and puffy eyes and the excuses were numerous as to why I looked as I did; allergies and a permanent cold were my usual lines of reason. I'm sure that those who knew me well enough could see I was hiding the truth but no-one pried.

Fragments of my heart had been left behind that day in the clinic and I barely had enough left to go on with life. My children kept me going and I would say kept me sane but the burden of guilt was so weighted it bared heavy down on my chest each morning when I opened my eyes to fearfully greet the day.

The ballet dancer came to visit for almost a year; such a long time to not know how to cope with such a mental image that destroyed me every single day. Everything became such an effort; a depression that swallows you up whole with no room to move or breathe. When I think back on that time, I can see actual darkness; images of night and a blackness that surrounded my life which gave a true metaphoric representation of living day to day and just existing.

I had not yet heard of Post Abortive Syndrome (PAS) but understand now that was the beginning of PAS and the road of destruction that I travelled on; that is until God and I went fishing again.

Chapter 11
Chocolate Cake

Job 10:8-12 "Your hands shaped me and made me. Will you now turn and destroy me? Remember that you molded me like clay. Will you now turn me to dust again? Did you not pour me out like milk and curdle me like cheese, clothes me with skin and flesh and knit me together with bones and sinews? You gave me life and showed me kindness, and in your providence watched over my spirit."

The first few months after the abortion left me dealing with self loathing and enjoying the daily punishments that I dished out to myself. My favorite mental beating would be imagining a chocolate birthday cake, presents, streamers and balloons; all the birthday things that my baby would not be able to have. I would bring the image so clearly into view that I could almost smell the warm chocolate baking in the oven and hear the laughter of the other children at the party; balloons popping, children screaming with exuberance and chairs being bumped into from all the running around, *but of course without the guest of honor.* My chocolate cake experiences were so very welcoming to me as they added more nails into my personal cross that I bore and carried. The weight of guilt felt good the heavier it became. I happily greeted the masochistic malevolence that I conjured up for my daily weigh in at the guilt factory.

Tracy Bihary

I would imagine the ballet dancer eating chocolate cake, smiling at me with sticky hands and melted chocolate splodges smeared around her mouth. She was always so happy, stretching to reach my hand and holding it tight. Chocolate cake became an item in the grocery isle that I couldn't bear to look at and I sadly never bought another chocolate cake until years later; the reality of an actual cake saddened me more than the imaginary cakes in my world of dreams.

The harsh world of real birthday parties that Brittany and Antony went to seemed to be forever tainted with stabs of rushing guilt that would swim over and engulf me to the point of suffocation. Seeing my children having fun; popping balloons, throwing streamers and eating birthday cake only saturated my mind even more to the baby that I'd thrown away who would never experience growing up or growing old. There would be no squeals of excitement as the happy birthday banner was put up in preparation for a party; there would be no exhilaration at ripping brightly colored wrapping paper from a gift and there would be no hugs and kisses or 'I love you's' to pleasure my soul.

Chapter 12
The Fetus

I Corinthians 6:19-20 "Do you not know that your body is a temple of the Holy Spirit, who is in you, whom you have received from God? You are not your own; you were bought at a price."

The ballet dancer became such a normal part of my day that I began to just expect her to be by my side every morning when I stepped outside my car. The guilt was not getting any better and daily my depression became worse. I began to assimilate everything relative to young children on television to the baby that I didn't have. Every commercial that advertised birthdays, parties, dresses and cakes was my time to dig the knife a little deeper into the wound that lay so widely open. Self torture is something that guilt enjoys. Masochistic would be the correct terminology for it; a self deprivation and degradation but something that is welcoming in the form of a self punishment for a crime committed and since I could not stand trial for murder, this was a way of living in my own prison.

Self loathing, guilt, anxiety and depression were common feelings to me every day. From sun rise to sun set I inwardly set about to mentally destroy myself as that is what I thought I deserved. I became a Jekyll and Hyde at my change in character so the children would not have to suffer my downward spiral, but I'm sure there were times they could see my sadness. I always put on my mask when they were around and tried to hide beneath the painted smiles and laughter. I enjoyed the children being with me as they were a distraction from my new life of wallowed misery; they gave me a reason to stay in the game and reminded me by their existence that I was a mother and they needed me to be whole and complete. Yet the journey was far from over and no rest bite existed from the guilt of my pain.

One particular Friday evening I had dropped the children off at their father's house for his weekend visitation and drove home in a somber mood, listening to 'The Piano' movie soundtrack by Michael Nyman. The haunting melody would take me on winding journeys of being with my sweet baby; sweeping me in and out of elf entrusted woodlands, magical colorful butterflies and gentle soporific running streams. Just briefly, I was able to spend harmonious moments of time being together with my baby in thoughts and images that belonged in a fairytale book. I constantly played the lingering music over and over that allowed my special time with her to exist.

I was about half way home when I thought I saw something out of the corner of my left eye. It was now summer and the evenings were long and warm but there was a cool breeze that night and my window was up to keep the drafty air out. I quickly turned my head and this time saw an aborted fetus pushing at the window trying to get into the car with me. Its wrinkled skin was covered in blood and its body was the size of a newborn baby!

I gasped and gripped the wheel to try and focus on the road ahead. My heart raced as I tried to breathe without hyperventilating. I had another ten miles or so to go and I needed to keep calm. Keep calm! How could I with that horrific sight in my mind! The light from the car seemed to prevent me seeing clearly outside the window but I had to look again and make sure that the fetus was not trying to get to me. I took a deep breath and quickly looked to my left, terrified of what I was going to see, yet the road was clear. The darkness began again to take on a deeper connotation than just in the night sky; the darkness was becoming my world. I began to cry and shake from fear; the resounding crescendos from 'The Piano' filled my ears with surging waves of melody and all I could see in my mind was the imprint of a fetus, my dead baby, trying to get in the car with me.

I managed to get home and spent a restless night afraid for my dreams and what they would bring. I left the light on in my bedroom which I did now all the time to ease the fear of the darkness and what I couldn't see and prayed to make it through until morning. Eventually I moved to sleeping on the sofa in the front room, the cushions were soft and I felt somehow comforted by the reminder of the first night I came home from the clinic. That was where I felt close to my baby.

Pray. Did I really pray? No, I still had not asked God to help me or save me from myself. I was entering a depth of depression that I didn't know how to control and living a double life of self mental destruction to my soul and a wonderful over achiever mother to my children; filling their days up with extracurricular activities and projects. I needed the world to see that I was a good mother. I was afraid that people would see through my disguise and so I marched on during the times that I was with my children as super-mom and fell to the pathetic, depressed and lost little girl when they were with their father every other weekend or asleep in their beds at home with me. Any time I was alone, I brought my new friends with me. Guilt, Anger, Depression, Anxiety and Psychosis as they were those I felt most deserving to be with.

The fetus returned to visit me a few more times; always whilst I drove alone wistful in my thoughts. I never thought of the fetus in any other way than sinister; it wasn't like the ballet dancer who would bring me some form of bizarre comfort, the fetus was seemingly angry and needed revenge. I would just see an image in my mind's eye outside the driver's window and in a split second it disappeared. I longed to tell someone of my living nightmare but I knew people would think I'd lost my mind and gone crazy. I wasn't insane; I was just living a double life of enormous guilt and sorrow against the normality of my days as mommy. PAS had taken a complete hold of my life.

Chapter 13
Cutting Hair

Isaiah 49:15 "Can a mother forget the baby at her breast and have no compassion on the child she has borne? Though she may forget, I will not forget you!"

I had begun to not take care of myself in appearance. I did the mandatory maintenance of cleanliness and dress code for the type of office position I held and had to continue toward a type of standard but I had lost the will to care enough how my hair looked; it had grown long and unkempt and it was worn screwed back pony tail with little or no makeup. I bought the children what I could afford and made sure that they looked nothing but well turned out, yet for myself, I didn't care what I looked like. I didn't deserve to look anything other than plain and most certainly did not deserve to pay attention to miner details such as nail polish or nice clothes.

One morning, I remember standing in my kitchen looking at the children's art work from school that I had hung along the top boarder. I suddenly grabbed all my hair in my hand, physically observing that it should all be cut off. Yes, cutting off all of it would be a punishment I was worthy of. I would look horrid and ugly. That would make me feel so much better! I could do it now; get the scissors and chop away but I let it go from my fingers and instead covered my face with my hands as I sobbed into despair to a heap of nothingness on the cold kitchen floor.

The punishment of my sin was seeping rapidly into my daily thoughts. I tried to find thoughts or actions that would make me feel even worse than I already did and sadly enough it felt good when I found a new chastisement to lengthen my inner prison sentence. I needed to endure retribution from my soul and mind. I needed to understand that the penalty for my sin was to just exist as my own life was not worthy to be saved.

More than anything, I needed help!

Chapter 14
Baby Socks

Mark 10:14 "Jesus said to them, 'Let the little children come to me, and do not hinder them, for the kingdom of God belongs to such as these."

Time moved on within the first year and I sunk lower into oblivion. My dual life was a hardship to endure and keep up; it was draining and so tiring. I knew that I had to somehow push forward and at least try to regain some of my soul. One particular day at work, I left lunchtime to go shopping trying to take my mind to living in the moment and not the constant past. I longed for the nightmare to end yet I enjoyed the deliverance of guilt no matter where I was or what I was doing. I entered the department store and wandered around, eventually ending up in the children's section to look at clothes for Brittany and Antony. But the baby section caught my eye and my legs swept me gently and effortlessly to the multitude of baby hats, bibs and socks. Oh how those socks burned my eyes. So wonderfully soft to the touch yet they were sharp and cut my very soul to shreds. I held the socks tightly imagining my baby's feet in the soft yellow material; kicking and gurgling with delight. I must have stood there for half an hour before I began to walk away to the cash register to buy the soft yellow socks. I carried them with me, always locked away in the side pocket of my bag and would bring the socks out from time to time to hold them and feel them close to my skin. I would allow moments of pure pleasure to rapture me as I imagined my baby in my arms wearing the yellow socks I'd bought, along with an imaginary yellow outfit and little yellow shoes. Those socks became my baby as PAS took me over completely. I'd tried to change and grasp on to the here and now, but just couldn't make any changes to my behavior and I guess the reality was, I didn't want to.

Chapter 15
The Pastor

Ezekiel 18:4 "For every living soul belongs to me, the father as well as the son—both alike belong to me."

The Holy Spirit had been challenging me; prodding me to want the God I knew in my youth. I needed Him to touch my soul and smooth away some of the pain that I had but it had been so long since I had asked Him anything. Early one morning after I'd dropped the children off at extended care for school I drove to a local church and sat outside in the car looking at the front door. I looked towards the steeple and the cross that hung reminding me that my baby was with the Lord. I knew that my baby was safe and loved; sitting at the feet of Jesus, listening to His stories full of wisdom and understanding. They were on a white cloud set against the bright blue sky and could look over the edge and see me just sitting there in the car. I began to cry. I wanted my baby with me.

I went to the church and opened the door; being early in the morning I didn't know if I could get in but a janitor was there and I asked if I could go and pray. I walked into the chapel and cast my eyes upon the stain glass windows that reflected such beautiful colors; Jesus on the cross, Mary praying at His feet and the Lord waiting for His son as my baby waits for me. My Lord, I had missed Him.

I sat on one of the benches and bowed my head in shame. I cried long, lonely tears and prayed for my baby that I wanted back so much; to touch, smell and see grow up enjoying all the chocolate birthday cakes in the world. I felt a peace within my soul; something that I hadn't felt for so long that I almost didn't recognize it; a stillness and quietness as only He can give you when He touches your heart and rests your mind.

The children and I began to go to church. I began to enjoy and look forward to Sundays, feeling God around me and feeling close to my baby. The children enjoyed it too and began to be our new routine at the end of a busy and full week. Yet one particular Sunday, my new found faith left as quickly as it had arrived. I had wanted to speak to the pastor and ask about forgiveness from abortion. I just needed to hear that although what I had done was wrong; that God forgave me and life would be okay again. But those are words that I did not hear.

I waited until the end of that Sunday's sermon and stood back in the foyer waiting for the pastor to finish mingling with her followers. I felt confident that being a female pastor, she would be the perfect person to talk to and understand how and why I felt the way I did. My eyes began to fill with tears; emotion getting the better of me as it always did. The children sat and waited patiently as I asked if I could speak with her. She smiled and ushered me into a side room.

"Thank you for speaking with me" I said nervously. "I wanted to ask about abortion. You see I had one a while ago and I want to know that I'm forgiven as it is such an evil thing to do. Abortion is so wrong and I feel so guilty!"

I pleaded with her silently for my sanity to be returned. I waited for the light of absolution or bells of release from my inner prison, but the response I received literally reeled me backwards in my chair; similar to a scene from Alice in Wonderland where everything is 'topsy turvy' and upside down. The room span and I felt sick to my stomach.

"Don't worry yourself my dear" she quickly replied. "I'm sure that if I had been in your shoes, I would have done the same thing."

Did I hear those words correctly? Was I now going mad? How could a pastor tell me that abortion was okay? Nothing made sense. I needed my Lord and my God to hold me; tell me I was okay and acknowledge that my sin was a sin and that it was over. What had just happened?

"What do you mean?" I asked. "Abortion is wrong!" I argued.

"Well, I believe there are some cases where it is okay and if I had been in your circumstances, I would have done the same as you." She smiled hoping that her answer had given me what I was looking for. Looking back, I pity the congregation of that church and what they were taught by such a misguided woman of the cloth.

Life didn't make sense anymore. Everything I'd been taught, everything I'd known to be true; even though I'd chosen to take a life, was now a complete contradiction to my entire world. I stumbled out of the pastor's office and ran from the church with my two children never to return. I was swimming in an ocean of evil and wickedness. Who could I turn to now? Even God's spokesperson could not redeem me.

Chapter 16
The Baby's Father

I Corinthians 1:27 " But God chose the foolish things of the world to shame the wise; God chose the weak things of the world to shame the strong."

I'm sure by now many of you are wondering what happened to the baby's father. Oh what a tangled web we weave! I've heard that expression so many times during my life and I've certainly made many webs that I've become tangled up in yet this one ended quickly as I let go and shut down the human emotion in me towards him.

As he had been such a main perpetrator in the decision for me to abort the baby, any feelings of love I'd had dwindled to nothingness. The life that I had planned for myself had diminished and with that nothing made sense anymore. At first my feelings turned to more of an absence of emotion, but over time that changed to anger and utter rage.

During the first months, I hid myself from everyone; the real me was inside crying out for help but no one could help or even see there was a problem. I became very good at hiding my emotion when in public or around others. I would not let anyone see what was truly evil inside; that I was a murderer and a killer and no good to anyone.

He had four children; two that he had partial custody for and two that he fathered but never saw. When I found out that I was pregnant and told him, the response I received was a blank and emotionless stare. Affordability was thrown into the mix and excuses of why not to have the baby and, that he could not take any financial support away from the two children that he already paid for; their extra-curricular activities and child support. But of course, he did however manage to offer and pay for an abortion.

I envied the mothers who had obviously had the courage to be single parents without him. Over time the rage turned into a wrath that I couldn't wash away and so the relationship ended. Nasty words and thunderous reactions came; I weathered the storm; he left my life and I never looked back. I pray that he has found the Lord and peace within his life.

PART TWO
THE LIGHT

Chapter 17
Post Abortive Syndrome

Romans 5:8 "But God demonstrates his own love for us in this: while we were still sinners, Christ died for us."

The physicality of mental decay is often worse than the reality of actual pain as mental anguish is debilitating and destructive to your psyche and soul. A physical impact and wound can be seen and addressed; there is evidence of contact relative to cause and effect yet, wounds of the mind are hidden deep behind pain that is invisible and concealed within memories. Thousands of people worldwide experience some form of depression and anxiety; much of which can be treated and often the cause determined, whether cultural or derived inherently, yet the struggle to prove the existence of PAS is an ongoing medical dilemma for those that know it exists against national organizations that speak of no evidence between abortion and mental health issues similar to post traumatic stress syndrome. Limitless studies relating to the evidence for PAS can be formulated and executed to gather data and output statistics yet many women do not come out of hiding from their internal mental hell for true studies to be taken. Through reading many research books and web sites it would appear that many statistics are taken from women who have had an abortion within the last five years and do not account for often a lengthy delay in showing PAS symptoms.

The debate of the existence of PAS will no doubt remain intact until the final battle is determined as to when life truly begins. That debate belongs in religion with those who flock to the Lord in His wisdom and love against those who choose to stand for women's rights and follow a path of sin and destruction. The combat and crusade for any debate relative to abortion will not be answered until the world unites in Christ. Yet, I know PAS exists and abortion is wrong as I experienced the most terrifying mental state of mind that I had no control over.

I was crying out for help.

Chapter 18
Christine

Psalm 86:5 "You are forgiving and good, O lord, abounding in love to all who call to you."

Life had moved on again and I was turning towards the end of my first year; troubled waters were engulfing me and I was trying to cope with depression, anxiety and guilt on a daily basis. I realized that my health was seriously deteriorating; all the stress that my body was enduring, the sleepless nights, the inner battle of 'happy mommy' for the children's sake against the sadness and crucifixion of my sins for my own twisted enjoyment of self destruction. It was all too much to bear anymore. I did not know who to talk to without being afraid of consequences or ramifications; would I be put on medication, would the children be taken away, would I be diagnosed insane? I was so terrified and scared of my next step yet I knew staying in the darkness would finally destroy me altogether and then the children would have no one to rely on at all.

It is quite incredible that people within Christ can read others trouble well enough to be helpful at just the right time. Divine intervention is a gift that the Lord gives by way of placing people in other's paths to help us on the way to salvation and this I believe the case to be for a kind friend at work who shared her faith with me. She had seen the tears in my eyes one morning and held my hand to ask me what

Tracy Bihary

was wrong. It was as if a green light went off in my head to say 'its okay, you can tell her'. Perhaps it was the Holy Spirit prodding me again. Christine was a blessing to my survival in many ways and through the brief yet full conversations we were able to share on her visits to the office, I was able to confide in her my sin and depth of agony.

I looked forward to her visits and longed for her grace, serenity and peace to engulf me. Her kind soul soothed my days as I shed all the past terrors to her of my abortion including the abuse and rape of previous years. She did not condemn me and shed no opinions other than those of God's word and His love. There is a saying that I came across; that people come into your life for a reason, season or a lifetime. Christine crossed my path for both a reason and a seasoned dose of help.

As a sales representative, Christine would frequently came into the office for supplies and I believe a caring excuse to see how I was. One particular day, not long after I'd shared my story with her she handed me a book "Her Choice to Heal; Finding Spiritual and Emotional Peace After Abortion" written by Sydna Masse and Joan Phillips. I was shocked that there was a book on my needs and that someone so kind could see my deep need of help! I looked at her through my glassy, watery eyes and mustered a smile for her through the internal fog surrounding me. She took my hand and asked if she could pray for me. Her words spilled out for my peace to be restored; for His love to reach me and comfort me, for my sins to be forgiven and my heart to be healed. As she spoke the words, I did not feel worthy of such kindness and sympathy. I still felt dirty and classed as a murderer but the warmth of her voice began to wash over me and for a moment I felt still. My head stopped spinning, my mind stopped racing with erratic thoughts and for a brief time, calmness and tranquility possessed my soul. There was a rest bite from the internal battle and war; freedom was in range and the spell of harmony lifted the darkness for a little while. I wanted to stay in that moment forever, a moment basking in His love and strength again.

The office provided a sanctuary for us that day; it was quiet, no managers or phone calls interrupted our brief time. We were in a secure bubble created by God for me to see what could be ahead and he had provided a messenger to save me from myself. Yet the journey was rigorously slow, long with winding roads and tall mountains; many times I pulled back from the fishing line that the Lord has cast out for me and fought against the current but Christine showed me the beginning of the road again and the start of my healing.

Wherever you are today Christine, I thank you for leading me into the path of the Lord again and on to the road of salvation and peace. I suppose it was a journey much as that was as Dorothy took in the Wizard of Oz. There was a starting point to that brightly colored road and it held many pitfalls along the way, but Dorothy returned to the home she loved, and I too have since returned to a complete soul. Christine, you are a warrior for Christ and one I will always remember. God Bless You.

Chapter 19
Self Healing Books

Titus 3:5 "He saves us, not because of righteous things we had done, but because of his mercy. He saved us through the washing of rebirth and renewal by the Holy Spirit."

The strength that I was given with Christine was enough to begin to look forward and I did so by reading the book she gave me. I read words that described my own feelings; I saw that I wasn't alone in my grief, anger and guilt and understood that other women had walked in my shoes feeling the pain of regret from terminating their baby. The comfort of not being alone was overwhelming. The knowledge that the feelings I had were part of abortion brought me back from the edge of insanity to be able to begin healing. The book from Christine became my bible; it went everywhere with me and I would reference it all the time.

As I read my new book, I understood that I wasn't alone and that my decision had been made as that of an animal caught in a trap, gnawing off its own leg trying to escape. This somewhat lessened the tremendous burden that I carried. I felt understood and validated in my grief as the book highlighted that the destruction of one's own child falls outside the scope of normal human experience and other emotions that I was feeling to a point of no return. I was able to level my thoughts to know that my journey to hell was understandable as I knew the value of human life and that to take action to end *any* life was the ultimate sin.

God became my carrier across the road to peace. I knew that I was far from that point and didn't know how the process should begin to find the permanent stillness that I yearned for. I read about guilt, anxiety, psychological episodes, anniversary patterns, re-experiences though flashbacks and many more symptoms that I lived as if I walked through a constant revolving door. I was relieved to read that reactive psychosis could occur causing the person who had the abortion to behave with a distorted view of reality; I didn't know to what degree I had experienced that, although I'm sure it was at a very high level, but it felt so comforting to read words that attested to my own delusional world that I had created.

One part of the book spoke to seeking a local pregnancy center that could help with any issues. I found myself seeking and searching new ways to confirm my behavior and confirm that what I had done was wrong; not just by my own standards but by Gods too. Finding others to agree to that became a very hard task as the idea of abortion sits on a fence; you are either for or against it. Roe versus Wade in 1973 had put the entire debate onto new grounds and the path for proving that abortion should be illegal continues to be a struggle. The next part of my healing process was about to begin. What fantastic marvels God is capable of; if we could just leave our burdens at the cross and have faith in Him.

Chapter 20
Cleveland Pregnancy Center

Romans: 1:7 "To all in Rome who are loved by God and called to be saints: Grace and peace to you from God our Father and from the Lord Jesus Christ."

What solace and peace you have given me. The Cleveland Pregnancy Center (CPC) deserves so many accolades for the help that it gives to those such as myself; lost in the world of grief, anxiety and depression from the affects of abortion.

The CPC began 1984 and is a life affirming organization that has helped many women along the path of healing from the aftermath of abortion. The center also assists those individuals who are pregnant and families who are in need of counseling through spiritual, emotional and physical guidance. They offer many programs that can equip and help those in need through a Christian path of recovery.

I walked into the Cleveland Pregnancy Center, scared of the unknown and mentally beaten down by the year of torture I had endured at my own hand. The building was small and somewhat hidden in a row of stores on a strip in Berea, Ohio. A little bell chimed as I opened the door to the reception room that felt warm and inviting. The light green walls were soothing and the wicker furniture felt relaxing; I was reminded of a spa that usurped tranquility and calmness. I stood for a minute looking round a room that would soon become my sanctuary.

"Can I help you?" came the soft voice from the end of the hallway.

I looked ahead and saw a very tender and warmhearted smile coming from a lady walking towards me and I instantly felt at peace. The softness in her eyes seemed to hold a world of answers that yearned for; as if an entrance to the door of the unborn had been opened. I was able to look and perhaps see as she did the light of the Lord everywhere around us; this place was my sanctuary, passage way and learning center for finding the quiet mind that I so needed.

"Come with me" she said looking into my hollow and sad soul, and I followed her into a room that emanated peace. Soft pastel colors draped my eyes and the high yielding energy that had been trapped in my body for so long began to dissipate into thin air. Calmness, tranquility and stillness were immeasurable feelings that covered my mind and body as I sat in the chair opposite my new found angel of hope.

She introduced herself and began to tell me about the center and what help they could give to people. Once she'd finished, the obvious question was asked.

"How can I help you?" Her words were soft and spoken as if she knew how broken I was inside. My story began and I unraveled all the horror that I had experienced since my abortion. The face in front of me took on a sympathetic understanding and sorrow; the related experience was something she had heard many times before, but I was treated and listened to as an individual in pain and need. Tears spilled over as I recounted the many terrors and demons that had willingly befriended me. I yielded to needing help and prayed that my journey of healing would be continued at the center through the HEART program that she spoke of.

Chapter 21
HEART

Week One
A New Beginning
Luke 4:18-19 "He has sent me to heal the brokenhearted and to announce that captives shall be released...and that God is ready to give blessings to all who come to Him."

So perfectly abbreviated! Healing the Effects of Abortion Related Trauma. I was home! I had found a new place to feel at peace within peers and with the Lord. The HEART program is for women who have experienced trauma from their abortion whether recently or years ago who can't forgive themselves, who don't know where to turn, and are in need of help by the way of the Lord. The program I attended was a seven week group workshop that provided a safe haven to talk, share and grieve the loss of children through abortion. There was a community feeling with those that shared the group's journey; a oneness and a wish to experience peace and forgiveness from God. I will never forget the women who shared my walk with the Lord during that time and hope that they are all still walking in peace with Him.

I began my first week at the center with nervousness; never having experienced a group healing session before and wondering what would lie in store for me with others who had also experienced abortion. Chairs were set up in a circle in the reception area of the office and once again that sense of peace engulfed me as I sat down. Others soon came in and the leader began our first session in prayer. I listened to the message of hope for us all to be healed and find peace within the Lord; I heard the words that I longed to hear, being asked on my behalf, as asking for myself to be forgiven and healed was a quest that I was far from being able to do. I sat and looked around the room at the women in the circle; there were no differences that I could see, they were women just like me, unsure and curious, afraid and yet somehow safe. We were asked to introduce ourselves to the group. Our words were few but each of us knew we would find each other through the weeks that lay ahead. Each one of us had a story inside; each one of us had forsaken a child, some multiple children and each of us were looking to end the struggle we faced each morning as the sun arose.

The leader of the group handed everyone a workbook that we would be using for the duration of our program. The front cover was of a heart which seemed to symbolize the endless love each of us had for our lost children and the way forward for recapturing peace. The word alone was a wonderful way to envelope so many wishes, feelings and desires and all of us sitting in that room had a heart full of healing needs.

As soon as the workbook had been placed in my hands my mind immediately began spinning in continuous circles trying to figure everything out. We began with reading testimonies of others who had travelled the HEART path; their words of encouragement and release of barriers to forgiveness held great encouragement towards our final destination; yet everything seemed so far away and even perhaps non-obtainable for me. I remember feeling that perhaps the women in the book had been more deserving of healing; that they walked a closer path with God and that He in His wisdom would know from this group who He could or could not forgive. I also at that time realized that even if I was able to receive His grace; I could never forgive *myself* for what I had done.

We moved onto the discussion of PAS and my soul exploded with joy! Listed in front of my eyes were lists of feelings and emotions due to unresolved psychological and spiritual needs. Oh the happiness in reading all of the terrible things that I had experienced! I was again validated for my emotions, feelings and behaviors throughout my painful ordeal and became elated that the noted symptoms of PAS were those that emanated my current life. We were asked to put a check mark against the specific feelings that we felt. I check marked almost all of them other than chemical or alcohol dependencies and blaming God. I sat and thought; blaming God. I had never once blamed God for my own actions. This was all me, my fault and my blame! It felt so enlightening to check mark my pencil against the long list of behavioral, emotional, and self worth problems that were listed. That was me! That was me! That was me! The twisted joy in finding ones broken entity that can be authenticated by endorsed PAS symptoms is immeasurable!

The group discussed each symptom listed and how we had developed each particular behavior into our lives. We were informed that obstacles would traverse our way as we moved into the path of healing from the Lord; obstacles from the devil who so delights in others pain and agony. It was to be a time of reliving the experience as we all worked through our journeys to salvation; reliving the experience was all that I did on a daily basis. I welcomed it.

The final task for our first week was in the form of a homework assignment; to write down our goals to have achieved by the end of the groups seven weeks together. My goals were to receive peace and inner healing; tear down walls to rebuild relationships with my parents, release my anger, stop crying near pregnant women or anything that was baby related and finally, to feel self worth again. A rather tall order of requests but I left the session feeling lighter and one step nearer to finding myself and the Lord again.

Chapter 22
Week Two

Defense Mechanisms and Anger
Psalm 27:1-3 "The Lord is my light and my salvation; whom shall I fear? The Lord is the defense of my life; whom shall I dread? When evil doers came upon me to devour my flesh, my adversaries and my enemies, they stumbled and fell. Though an army may encamp against me, my heart will not fear; though war may arise against me, in spite of these I shall be confident."

The week that followed was long and labor filled with work commitments. I couldn't wait for the next HEART session and a chance to move forward even more in my healing. Soon enough the day arrived and I wondered if all the ladies I had met the week before would be there. Perhaps some were frightened and were not ready for healing to take place. I knew I was ready although still unsure of what lay ahead but my footsteps felt light as I walked into the room and sat down with the leader in our safe circle. The ladies started arriving and everyone from the week before came. I was so pleased and happy to see everyone again. These women were my new family, a group of souls that were torn down soon to be put back together again.

Once we were all seated, we opened in prayer. Hearing words spoken to the Lord for our group to be blessed and for each one of us to find peace brought tears to my eyes. The anxiety that I carried every day fell from my shoulders for that brief time with the group and I felt the arms of the Lord wrap around us. After the prayer we discussed our homework of what we all wanted to achieve when we left the groups fold. Most of us said the same thing in one way or another. We were all walking the same path and wanted the peace to reign in place of the evil we felt every day.

We spoke of defense mechanisms that many women experience which are methods used to deal with the stress and trauma of the abortion. I listened to each one being discussed; repression, suppression, rationalization, denial; all words to make believe that having an abortion or forgetting about it was okay. Yet I couldn't really identify with any of them as I had known immediately as I awoke in the abortion clinic that what I had done was by my own hand and was wrong on every conceivable level. I hadn't ever avoided the subject; I'd deliberately driven towards it every day, seeking out the memories of my actions over and over again.

We moved on to discuss fears, anxieties and anger that women can experience after abortion. This was a topic for me to spread my wings in and explore. Fear! Anxiety! Anger! Oh yes, that was me; all day and every day! We were asked to make a list of feelings that were experienced on a frequent basis and as I look back on that list today I feel so much compassion for the lost person that I was back then. The feelings I had described in my workbook were of being heartbroken, inadequate and empty. Oh how empty I was; just a shell of a person who had become two people in one; the happy mommy for the children, and the other a sad and empty woman with hollow and empty eyes that held no soul.

I had never blamed anyone else for my own actions, but I'd held a great deal of anger inside me against those that I'd felt lead me down the path to abort my baby. I'd been angry with my parents, my boyfriend and his entire family. The irony was that his family had never known about the baby as my boyfriend hadn't wanted me to discuss any of the pregnancy or abortion with them at all. But most of all, I was angry at myself for not having the courage and guts to stand up and stand alone and fight for my unborn child. As I sat and reflected on my anger I saw how bitter I'd become; inwardly destroying me and my existence and the normality of living a happy life with my children. Yet letting anger go is a hard task and takes a leap of faith within the Lord; anger is a key to understanding who we need to forgive in our life. Ephesians 4:31-32 says to 'get rid of all bitterness, rage and anger, brawling and slander along with every form of malice; be kind and compassionate to one another, forgiving each other, just as in Christ God forgave you.' These words are so true, yet, forgiveness is an action that requires so much strength as it is so much easier to hate and be angry with someone than to let them go with forgiveness. I wasn't there yet. I knew that God would forgive me if I asked for his forgiveness, but I had never felt worthy of that and I thought I could never accept forgiving myself for what I had done. I had trouble forgiving my boyfriend and most of all I so desperately wanted to forgive my mother and father.

As we wrapped up the session, we were given our homework assignment for the week. We were to list our defense mechanisms, fears and with whom we were angry. I remember that week wondering what my defense mechanisms really were as I couldn't see any but then I realized that my entire being had become super independent. I had become a sole entity in my lost time of living; I'd made a point of never wanting to depend on anyone else again. I had put up walls through my anger and had fought a long battle to contain my sanity. I'd over compensated with the children when I was 'happy mommy' by taking them to every conceivable afterschool activity possible; karate, dance, baseball, swimming to give them everything that I'd taken away from the baby. I had buried myself so far in guilt that I was swimming like a duck; paddling like crazy under the water just to stay afloat.

Chapter 23
Week Three

Forgiveness
Jeremiah 31:34 "For I will forgive their iniquity and their sin I will remember no more."

Week Three entered into the world of forgiveness and the one area that I seemed to be having the most difficulty with. I understood that forgiveness meant letting go and perhaps that was one reason why I didn't want to forgive. I still felt so entwined with my actions and letting them go would have left me in a new and vulnerable world. I knew where I was in the middle of my turmoil, grief and guilt that I loaded onto my shoulders every day. It was a punishment that I looked forward to giving myself when I woke up because I wasn't worthy of 'forgiveness' and I had not wanted to forgive anyone else for their hand in my abortion.

How arrogant was I! When I look back to know that God would forgive me but that I wouldn't forgive myself! Did I think that I was greater than God in who should or should not be forgiven? No, I believe that I just felt safe and comforted by my sad world that I existed in.

Yet here I was; I needed to break free and needed to follow instructions to forgive those that had trespassed against me and even forgive myself. It was the key to my freedom and shackles around my life.

Tracy Bihary

I looked at the group as we sat down after our opening prayer and wondered how forgiveness played in their
lives. As we discussed our issues, it appeared that I wasn't
the only one who had struggled with the subject; in fact,
most of us reached the problem of forgiving ourselves. A
natural issue it seemed for if one has a conscience and one
knows that a behavior or action committed is wrong; it can
be the hardest thing in the world to say 'I'm forgiven' that is
unless you fully believe in Christ.

The bible is full of verses that speak of forgiveness; the
subject is one of the foundational principals of the Christian
faith yet unless you surrender yourself fully to the teachings
of the Lord, obey his words and follow his path and exam-
ple, any lack of forgiveness will eat you alive. To be able to
forgive is such a hard action as it stems from a raw passion
of anger and self righteousness that are emotions that like
to stand on their own terms.

I struggled with the class that week and spoke up
about my doubts. I couldn't grasp and fully understand that
God would forgive me and that I could learn to move on. I
wanted His forgiveness but I had lived so long in my darkness that I was afraid to let it go. To forgive myself would
take so much more. The answer was in my grasp but yet
so far away! I told the group that I liked the weight of guilt
that led me through my life. The teacher understood and
expressed it in a way that I have always remembered so
well, as it described in a very simple way what I did every
morning. She looked at me with a kind smile and explained,
'...you put a back pack on when you get out of bed and load
it with every negative emotion you can find. The weight of
that back pack is the reminder of what you did and some-

72

thing that you don't want to let go of. But you must begin to take out the bricks of guilt, anger, depression and sadness to be able to live your life again. The Lord will be with you through your journey Tracy.'

We were then taken on what would be one of the most poignant moments of the entire HEART program. We were encouraged to think of our baby as a person and give them a name. The teacher explained that being able to let go of someone cannot really be complete unless they are a complete person to start with. It made sense but the reality of a name brought the entire forgiveness of abortion into a new light. I closed my eyes and thought of the prettiest name that I had heard; Savannah came to my mind. The majestic and breathtaking Savannah plains in Africa were a place that I had always wanted to visit. I imagined the magical and enchanting morning mists, hot days and cool, soft evenings, just as captivating as Savannah my baby would have been. My baby now had a name and the relief of emotions flooded through me as she was now whole and complete with the Lord.

Later on that evening, I sat with the children and just watched them from an inner view; Brittany and Antony, wonderful loving children that I'd named with purpose. Brittany as it reminded me of Great Britain and Antony after Marc Antony, strong and courageous in battle. I realized that all my children had names except the two I had lost through miscarriage. I sat and thought of who those babies were and what their names would be. Nathanial John and David Caleb were the names I decided on. I'd had five children; three of whom were with the Lord and I loved and missed them terribly.

Tracy Bihary

Our homework that week was to write letters to those that we needed to forgive. The letters were to be kept and not sent but used in a form of therapy to put down our thoughts and let go of the burdens that we carried around. I sat and pondered on the possibility of forgiving all those that had played a part in my abortion. I thought writing letters to everyone would be so difficult. How wrong I was!

Chapter 24
Book of Letters

I John 4:8 "Whoever does not love does not know God, because God is love."

I have been taught that the writers of the Bible are the Lords vessels by which He speaks to us. That the pens used in early scrolls were directed from God and that He spoke through his prophets. I believe that the Holy Spirit descended upon my pen and the words that I had so long struggled for were released into the following verses. The Lord was with me as I began the homework of writing my letters of forgiveness. Following are poems that I termed a Book of Letters. The opening verse is a different version of the Lord's Prayer.

Tracy Bihary

❧❧

Our father who art in Heaven
Forgiving be thy name
The gift you gave
We took away
On earth—may they rest in Heaven
Give us this day
Your gracious hand
And forgive us our trespasses
As we try to forgive ourselves for our sins
And lead us never down that road again
And deliver us from the enemy
For thyne is the Kingdom
The father of our children
Forever and ever
Amen

❧❧

৵৵

(Baby's letter to God)
How Grand
How grand it would have been God
To dance in fields of green
To run and laugh at marigolds
What fun it would have been

How grand it would have been Lord
To feel my mother's kiss
Her soft warm breath across my brow
To feel unending bliss

How grand it would have been God
To see the world you made
To take away my mother's pain
For such a price she paid

How grand it would have been Lord
To wipe away her tears
Instead she looks for shadows
Holds on to emptiness and fears

How grand it would have been God
To hold her hand in mine
I try to tell her where I live
The sun will always shine

Tracy Bihary

How grand it would have been Lord
To hug my daddy tight
Please tell him we forgive him
With a kiss from me at night

How grand it would have been God
To play on Grandpa's knee
Please tell him we forgive him
Let his heart and soul be free

How grand it would have been Lord
To hold my nana near
Please tell her we forgive her
Blow the clouds away and fear

How grand it would have been Lord
To see my mother's face
But I'll be there to welcome her
Upon her resting place.

Chocolate Cake In Heaven

❧

(God's letter to Baby)
Mommy's Forgiveness
Come my little one, sit with me
And I will just explain
Why mommy doesn't feel the sun
She wants to feel the rain

She's holding on for comfort
Of the things that could have been
For all you would have done in life
For all you would have seen

Mommy feels so empty
As she took your life away
And wants to suffer with her guilt
She carries every day

But she knows that I forgive her
It's herself she can't forgive
It's not enough for mommy
It's the way she wants to live

She feels there's one way open
To atone for what took place
To stop another death
Take the pain and wash her face

79

Tracy Bihary

To help another mommy
Not make the same mistake
So they can see their own child
Sit and eat their chocolate cake

She knows my son who died for you
Died for her own sins too
But I will let your mommy
Do the things that she must do

And one day when her time is here
You'll meet her at the gate
And watch her smile, It will be done
No longer will she wait

Chocolate Cake In Heaven

శ్రీ

(Mommy's letter to God)
Fields of Light
Thank you for the gift you sent
The life I bore within
I took away the joy you gave
The ultimate one sin

I know that she is with you
And runs in fields of light
I know that you forgive me
But I have an inner fight

The loss, the grief, depression
Is often more that I can bear
And though you try and take the guilt
It's something I won't share

I know this isn't something
That I'm leaving up to you
But I hope I have your blessing
For the fight I have to do

I'm sorry Lord for what I did
A mistake from no return
To hold her in my arms
Is such a feeling that I yearn

Tracy Bihary

One day when I am with you
Let her be there at that place
So I can feel her kisses
Wash my soul and kiss my face
ক—ক

Chocolate Cake In Heaven

಄

(God's letter to Mommy)
Rest Assured
Rest assured that I forgive you
You know it in your heart
And for some years you will await
And have to stay apart

Rest assured that she is with me
Savannah I hold high
She twinkles in the stars at night
The sun that's in the sky

Rest assured she is my angel
Like her sister there with you
Savannah is my ray of light
For all that she will do

Rest assured you have my blessing
In your journey now to save
Another baby from its death
A spirit from the grave

So go my child and know you're blessed
With all you have to say
So come to me with questions
And together we will pray

಄

Tracy Bihary

❧❧
(Mommy's letter to Baby)
Pigeons
You complete my book of letters
They're my testament to you
I carry you forever
Every day in all I do

How could this have happened?
I save pigeons from their doom
And yet I put my child to death
Within that cold dark room

Savannah how I miss you
Wish to hold you, kiss your lips
Brush your hair and dress you
Touch you with my fingertips

How I love you more than you could know
Regret what I have been
And wish upon the star you are
For all you would have seen

Candle flames and rushing winds
I see you in my mind
But you are with Our Father
Who is merciful and kind

Chocolate Cake In Heaven

The Christmas plays and parties
Ice cream fudge and chocolate cake
Coloring and tying shoes
School projects we could make

Know that one day when I see you
My arms will open wide
I'll hug you tightly darling
No more shame I'll ever hide

We will laugh, sing songs, read stories
Sleep together, softly sigh
For no more tears will spill my face
And no more will I cry

Sleep my baby, wait for me
Your blanket fit for two
Your wings they sparkle gently
Oh Savannah, I love you!

৵৽

My letters were complete and so was the first part of my journey. Relief flooded through me as I let go of the anger and bitterness that I had held in for so long. God and I had been conversing and he knew what I wanted to do, yet as always, everything that we want only happens if He deems it possible and in His time frame not ours. My healing was far from complete and I still had a very long journey ahead of me but I knew that I was forgiven from the Lord, that I had forgiven those that had trespassed against me and though I strived daily to forgive myself, I knew it would be the last step that I needed to complete.

Chapter 25
Week Four

God's Grace, Mercy and Peace
Psalm 25:18 "Look upon my affliction and distress and take away all my sins."

Life was becoming less surreal and less stressful. I was learning to be a mother again without the dual personality of happy and sad mommy; learning to cope with life once more and understand the Word of the Lord. I could go to work and not continuously douse myself in the shower of negativity that had been my ritual daily cleansing.

Week four held a new experience in the group for me. I still had my misgivings about my own forgiveness but I was getting there and the light at the end of the tunnel was brighter. Week four centered on God's Grace, Mercy and Peace. Grace is the word used for His richness in forgiveness, mercy and compassion. Heart described Grace as a pardon for sins and denoted each letter of Grace to God's Righteousness At Christ's Expense. We studied scripture passages during our session; passages that described the love of God and His mercy to all of us.

I looked at the women in my group with whom I'd become a family to. We all nestled in the center and purpose of receiving forgiveness through a divine God who was watching over all our babies together. We were all a unit and through our journey together had become close. I loved my sisters who understood me and I them.

I remembered when I had my first child Brittany. I had been walking through the town pushing her in the stroller. I distinctly remember the sun shining so brightly that day and the warmth of it covering my skin. As I walked I noticed other mothers with their children and I felt a special kinship with them; an unspoken understanding that we belonged to a sacred membership of affinity. I had the same again feeling sitting amongst my peers at HEART. We all needed and were growing in the love, grace, mercy and peace of the Lord.

My tension in life was diminishing but it was still a struggle in the mornings when I woke up as I had lived so long with so much guilt that the same evil would flood through me for an instant until I pushed through the mire to seek my God who was holding my baby. If you do something one way for so long, it becomes second nature and a normal pattern, almost like a learned response; the old days of Pavlov's Dog that I'd studied in school, whose behavior was one of repetition. Once I found myself and gathered my thoughts into a new way of thinking; letting go of the negativity, I relaxed and calmed my brain from images of scrambled eggs to the Lord sitting in Heaven with my little one at His feet.

Chapter 26
Week Five

Depression, Guilt and Grief
Psalm 32:1, 2, 5 "Blessed is he whose transgressions are forgiven, whose sins are covered. Blessed is the man whose sin the Lord does not count against him and in whose spirit is no deceit. Then I acknowledged my sin to you and did not cover up my iniquity. I said, "'I will confess my transgressions to the Lord.'"—and you forgave the guild of my sin.

If only we could live in Christ permanently and feel secure in His love we would not be influenced to breathe in the evil of depression, guilt and other negative emotions. Perhaps some do, but I would frequently fall short of God's ways. He was there and I found Him when I looked, but the devil would sit on my shoulder and come along for the ride, badgering me and knocking at my door of ultimate salvation. I could hear him throwing negative words at me constantly, and I would fight the good fight to regain self control and try to remember that my Lord was always with me no matter what.

Living through the abortion experience and trying to live a new life was hard. Imagine a scale that would constantly swing up and down. The upside to the journey was that at least now there was an up. In the group we were reminded that this was a long and arduous voyage and there would be times of sadness and feelings of helplessness. But we were moving forward; onwards and upwards and our lives were richer for it.

We opened in prayer and then began talking about the depression, guilt and grief that would still overwhelm us at times; a natural response to physical or mental pain that was too much to cope with or foster a solution to. Week five was an exploratory session through the stages of each negative emotion and was a wonderful way to understand why and how we trek the paths of destruction.

Our homework that week was to memorialize our babies in a special and meaningful way. There were many suggestions of how that should be done; either by a letter, a special painting, a song or a tree to grow. I had written my letters to God and Savannah but a memorial was a seal and assurance of love and forgiveness; another way that healing could flourish within all of us in the group. I decided to use the Certificate of Dedication that was also in the handbook for the group to use. The simple message was to certify that Savannah would be presented to the Lord in a dedication ceremony when the group next convened. I couldn't wait for the next week to arrive.

Chapter 27
Week Six

Dedication Service
Proverbs 3:5-6: "Trust in the Lord with all your heart and lean not on your own understanding; in all your ways acknowledge him, and he will make your paths straight."

Now that Savannah had taken on a reality more than I could have ever thought possible, I was able to relate all the experiences I'd had of seeing her as a ballet dancer and feeling her presence with me. She is a person; real flesh and blood and safe in the arms of Christ. I missed her so much and wanted her more than I could bear. I ached for the little bundle that I could have held and showered with kisses.

I was looking forward to seeing my new friends for our dedication service and took my certificate to proudly read her name out loud. The group met and opened in prayer. We began with talking about Self Reconciliation through forgiveness; an area that still swept me up in so much negativity. I looked at my certificate and felt a sense of peace and even tranquility as I was honoring my child to the Lord.

We began in our circle discussing what each of us had done to memorialize our children. One lady had made a beautiful picture and framed it with her sons name on it. Several within the group had also decided upon the certificate and as we each read our children's names we prayed with such reverence of love and peace that we each had been able to receive upon our special journey with the Lord.

At the end of the service we were told of a wonderful surprise. Our babies' names were to be put on a commemorative plaque to be hung on the wall at the Cleveland Pregnancy Center. Savannah's name is still on the wall today and I touch her name with a kiss whenever I visit.

Chapter 28
Week Seven

Committal to the Lord Service
Romans 12:2 "And do not be conformed to this world, but be transformed by the renewing of your mind, that you may prove what the will of God is, that which is good and acceptable and perfect.

Habits are hard to break. Negativity can envelope you if you have trained yourself to think a certain way for so long and a constant battle wages with the devil and how he can weave into your thoughts and create havoc. If you let the devil get just one minute of your time in entertaining the negativity, you can spend hours undoing the mess that is created.

I spent the week feeling so much more at peace with myself but as far as I'd come in my journey, I still allowed myself the liberty of feeling depressed and hating myself for what I'd done; keeping myself in bondage. The arrogance of knowing that God forgave me but needing the negativity to remind me that what I'd done was wrong had become ingrained in my soul. It was something that needed to be addressed and disappear forever. My prayers were answered at the last meeting we had.

The group was asked to meet at Grace Church in Middleburg Heights rather than our usual retreat at the Cleveland Pregnancy Center. I had not been to Grace before but felt a wonderful peace and serenity as I entered the building. The group was taken to a beautiful room with flowers on the wall and offered to sit in comfy chairs that had been placed in a circle. We opened in prayer and prayed for the group in the Committal service that we were to undertake that evening; a service that would release the babies from our tortured minds to the peace that lay within the arms of the Lord.

We were each asked to take a balloon and write the name of our baby on it. I understood that at this moment I was going to let Savannah go from my hold of negativity and sadness and be free from my own hell on earth that I'd created.

It was such a bright and sunny early evening. There was a special warmth in the air; the sun gently covered my face and tears of love and joy fell down as we said a prayer and let our balloons go into the gentle breeze. We watched them for a long time until they disappeared from our view. It was done. My guilt was released and my baby Savannah looked down at me with smiling eyes as she lay in the arms of her savior. It is so wonderful that such a simple symbol of a balloon could have helped me so much. I had finally begun to forgive myself.

Chapter 29
Dad

I Chronicles 16:34 "Give thanks to the Lord, for he is good; his love endures forever."

My parents had never known that I'd held such animosity towards them, we never spoke about the abortion yet that was all I'd ever thought about when I had spoken to them on the phone. It was a subject that had been pushed under the carpet and kept hidden like dust. I feared that my relationship with them would completely diminish if I did not make an attempt to say how I felt. I'd been wounded by the two people that I loved and adored by their own fear and endless love for me; I needed to re-open the wound face to face and fix the problem.

I decided to take a vacation home to England with the children. It had been two years since I'd been home and I felt distant and unwelcome when the plane landed. I needed to remind myself that I was still at the beginning of a journey of healing and so many new emotions were attacking me and shaking the foundation of the person that I had become. I was happy to be back in my home country but then afraid. I felt unsure of myself, vulnerable and scared of what I needed to do.

My father came to pick me up from the airport and I remember the ride home being very tense and uncomfortable. All I wanted to talk about was the baby that was thrown away; the life that was extinguished by my hand, the grandchild that they so readily gave up on, but all we spoke of was the weather and what was going on in the news. I was tired from the flight and the children were exhausted. I looked out onto the blue-gray colored ocean and at the waves lapping at the shore. My parents retirement home was lovely; a cottage by the sea with the white picket fence and beautiful flower garden. The sun caught the tops of the waves and the white surf gently splashed down onto the next wave that had gone before it. My home; I had missed it.

I looked at my father's aged face. He had been very ill, suffering a heart attack a few years previously and was on a great deal of medication to regulate his body. He was a 'medical marvel' so the hospital said and I had to agree with everything that he had physically gone through. I was unsure of saying anything to upset him. I held back from conversation yet tried to wait for an opportunity to bring up the subject before we arrived home. The sticky words and short responses that I gave from his questions must have confused my father until I could bear it no more and I told him to park the car along the side of the road.

I looked out onto the glistening sea and tried to formulate a sentence but the words would not come. "What is it sweetheart?" asked my dad in a concerned voice. I looked back at the children who were sleeping and then whispered, "The baby dad!" and I began to cry. "You don't understand that I killed my own baby! Technically I'm a murderer!"

My father looked sad and said in a soft voice "No you didn't, it was the right thing to do at the time."

Oh why was it so difficult for people to understand that abortion is wrong and that every single day innocent babies are killed? Why couldn't my father acknowledge what I was saying?

"Dad! When are you going to understand? What I did was wrong and I need you and mom to understand that!"

He looked at me for a moment and nodded as if he understood my plea. "Okay, let's get home and talk to your mother."

Chapter 30
Mom

John 16:27 *"...the Father himself loves you because you have loved me and have believed that I came from God."*

I had missed my parents yet the uncomfortable relationship that I had created had become so destructive in my outlook to them. Phone calls that had been made had been short and to the point. I had become silent since the abortion with little communication and had let my mother do the talking, yet inside my head I'd been screaming at her to hear me. I hugged my mother with all the love I'd been bottling up and keeping from her and looked around the house that I so fondly remembered. The children excitedly ran outside to the garden and then down onto the beach to play. My time was now; my time had come to tell my mother what I felt.

"I need to talk to you" I said. "I've already told dad but I need to read something to both of you". I took out my book that Christine had given me from my purse and without saying anymore, began to read lyrics from the song 'A Baby's Prayer' by Kathy Troccoli that I had found within the pages of my new bible. To this day, these words will bring tears to my eyes but now the tears are with the knowledge that my little one is with the Lord. When I read this to my parents my grief and sadness was overwhelming; here I was bearing my soul to them and I prayed that the Lord would reach into their hearts and souls to give them His eyes to see that abortion is wrong.

෮෧

I can hear her talking with a friend
I think it's all about me
O how she can't have a baby now
My mommy doesn't see
That I feel her breathe
I know her voice
Her blood, it flows through my heart
God, you know my greatest wish is that
We'd never be apart

But if I should die before I wake
I pray her soul you'll keep
Forgive her Lord—she doesn't know
That you gave life to me
Do I really have to say good-bye?
I don't want this time to be through
Oh please tell her that I love her Lord
And that you love her too
On the day that she might think of me
Please comfort her with the truth
That the angels hold me safe and sound
Cause I'm in heaven with you

෮෧

I looked at my mother waiting for a reaction and watched her face crumble before me. The worn lines in her face deepened and her happiness to see me faded to shock and fear. I saw the recognition in her eyes of what she and my father had done and been a conscious party to; I watched as her tears began to cascade down her face and saw her body drop to kneel at my feet.

"God forgive me. What have I done!" she pleaded. "I'm so sorry, I'm so sorry" were the words she cried over and over again.

I looked at my father who was gently sobbing; sitting in his comfy chair with his worn hands covering his face. I had succeeded! My elation at their agony was the best relief I could have ever asked for and yet my pity for them groaned in me as I had felt their pain every day since I'd let my baby go.

The remainder of my visit was joyous and full of love and affection as a united family. I told them of the HEART program and how I had been able to forgive myself for the life I had taken. It was a time of healing for all of us and a time we could join together in God's never ending love for his children. God had worked His miracle and brought us together again to worship Him in His glory.

Chapter 31
My Testimony

Matthew 5:4 "Blessed are those who mourn, for they shall be comforted."

Five years had passed by and I had lived a new life of worshiping and serving the Lord. I had been able to become whole again and be the mother that my children needed, taking care of them without a dual life of sadness and guilt. I thought of Savannah every day, and still do, but with a peace and comfort that has taken the place of all the negative emotions I use to feel. I had forgiven myself for the act of abortion and found safety and love in the arms of Christ. The Lord had also brought Dwane into my life with his son Christopher and we were married in November 2003. We were a new family starting out on a new journey.

I had attended Grace Church as my parish church since HEART had brought me there with Savannah. The warmth and grace of the church was a home from home and it was where I associated my baby with the Lord. I knew she was there every time I entered the building. I sensed her and felt comforted in God's house with my baby in His arms.

January 2005, I asked the pastor if I could give my testimony on Right for Life Sunday. I needed to tell my story with the hope to impact someone into not making the same mistake that I had made so many years ago. My request was joyously accepted and I set to compiling a brief synopsis of what you are reading. I entitled the testimony My Back Pack and condensed the message into a few minutes. The last few paragraphs are as follows:

I had chosen the name Savannah and wrote it on my balloon, and also Grace—for the Grace of Jesus Christ had freed my soul and spirit and it was the name of the church that she was sent from.

Today, I am the assistant teacher on Wednesdays in the 3 year olds room. Today, my family and I attend Grace Church. My children are part of the youth ministries and my new husband has reformed his walk with the Lord. I am so blessed to be free from my guilt and I am reminded daily when I take my children to school and they carry their back packs, how I don't need mine anymore.

I urge any of you that are in pain from the trauma of abortion or know of someone in need—to seek help from a Christian organization such as HEART, that can equip you, or them with the tools of Jesus to help you find peace.

The Lord is so good to us—he has been good to me.

Telling my story was a cleansing act for me and a step towards preventing more needless abortions. I gave my testimony three times that Sunday and would have gladly spoken through another 3,000 services in the hope of reaching any lost soul such as I had been.

PART THREE
THE GIFT

Chapter 32
The Gift

Hebrews 13:5 "…I will never desert you, nor will I ever forsake you."

The years moved on and I was now forty-two. I had been in hospital a few times with ovarian cysts and endometriosis and both my husband and I had resigned ourselves that we would not be able to have any more children. Having another child had been something that we had wanted a couple of years after we were married but we had never been successful. The continuing health problems and my age were just against all possibilities of conceiving and I was okay with God's decision for me not to have any more.

My abortion had also been meaningful for my husband as he too had gone through a journey of two of his children being aborted. Often men are left out of the equation or do not perhaps see the depth of despair that can be caused by the act, however, my abortion had brought him to recognize that his aborted children were with the Lord, watching over him and waiting patiently, as all aborted children do, for their parents to come home and be reunited.

We were due to go on our first actual family vacation. We had not all been able to go away at the same time before; being step family meant that other family commitments took us all in different directions, but we had saved our money to be able to spend a week at Bald Head Island resort which is at the southern tip of North Carolina. I had

Tracy Bihary

not felt well a few days before and came down with the flu;
taking over the counter medication to feel better and enjoy
the holiday with the family. We arrived on the island looking forward to our whirlpool hot tub that would be in our
vacation rental yet the night before we arrived, a storm had
blown through the island and had taken out the windows of
the property that we were to have for that week. We were
all so very disappointed; the hot tub had been the highlight
of what we wanted to be a relaxing holiday. After much de-
liberating, we were told there was no other property that
we could have with a hot tub but an equivalent property in
size would be available.

The week away was wonderful. Everyone was able to
rejuvenate their batteries even though it had been cold and
windy during March; the 'off season'. Regardless of the lack
of sun, the children had a marvelous time and it remains
today my all time favorite vacation spot.

Life returned back to normal and my flu dissipated as
quickly as it came yet I had been left with a nasty heartburn
that would not go away. The pain continued to the point
that I thought perhaps I had an ulcer and I went to the
hospital for tests to be run. Great I thought more health
problems!

During the next few days that I waited for the hospital
results, I also had stomach cramps. I was waiting for my
menstrual cycle and yet it wouldn't come. Day after day I
waited and still nothing.

"Do you think you are pregnant?" my husband asked
me candidly.

"Oh, absolutely not!" I assured him laughing in disbelief at the question. I had stomach pains and felt that at any minute my period would start.

The following day I thought on what my husband had asked me. Pregnant? I couldn't be! I was forty-two and had reproductive issues, yet I continued to have heartburn and then it hit me! I'd had dreadful heartburn with Brittany when I was pregnant but that was only in the third trimester. It surely wasn't the same, was it?

At work the next day I watched the clock on my computer slowly churn the time until lunch hour arrived. I drove to the pharmacy in somewhat of a pensive mood and bought a pregnancy test kit. I put it on the car seat next to me on the way back to work, glancing at it; could I be? It couldn't be possible. I wasn't late in my menstrual cycle—or was I? I wasn't usually out on my dates, especially since having all the reproductive issues I'd had.

I took the test and waited for the three minutes to go by; three minutes that felt like three years! I watched and waited whilst the clear strip slowly moved across the 'view window'. My head was spinning with concepts of what the outcome could be. I just knew that I could not possibly be pregnant.

......and it was positive!

Chapter 33
The Baby

"My Lord, you gave me back the gift I so carelessly through away! What did I do to deserve this God? I'm forty-two and pregnant; will the baby be okay? If not; if I have a Down Syndrome baby I will love it my Lord. I don't care if the baby is disabled or if there is something wrong with it! You gave a baby back to me and I know it is a girl."

These were the words and thoughts that ran over and over in my mind! My husband was elated as was the rest of the family. Brittany would be eighteen, Chris would be eighteen, Antony would be sixteen and they would have a little baby sister! What did I do to deserve this miracle?

I thought how the Lord had protected me during our vacation as hot tubs are not advisable to pregnant mothers. He had made sure that this gift was safe within my body, growing healthily every day. I called my parents and told them the news. Memories came flooding back of the last time that I'd told them that I was pregnant; the terror they had felt, the upset and fear, but I knew that this time it would be different.

My mother broke into tears and said she now finally felt forgiven and in the background on the telephone, I heard my father scream in delight!

The first few weeks passed and my nerves of losing the baby were terrible. I couldn't concentrate on anything and feared the worst all the time. I'd been given this gift and I didn't want to lose it! But one morning on the way to work, driving down the same freeway where I'd seen the posters against abortion so long ago, I heard God's voice speaking to me; very plain and simple words that washed over me with love.

"Be still" He said; just two words that told me that everything would be alright. I trusted the Lord and rested my weary mind from overloading again and worrying about something that was out of my control. I listened to Him and I was still.

My ultrasound was scheduled for May of 2007. Dwane and Brittany came with me as they wanted to see the sex of the baby but I already knew, and had my heartfelt conviction of a little girl verified on the monitor. There she was; God's miracle! Gwenyth Georgia Margarette Bihary.

I took a silent moment and spoke to Savannah in prayer.

"My precious baby, how I miss you and wish you could be with me. You will never be replaced in my heart; for you are equal with all my children on earth and in heaven. When it is your birthday we will eat cake and you can have your chocolate cake in heaven. When you next see the Lord, please thank Him for the gift he gave back to me. I love you!"

Chapter 34
Full Circle

Genesis 28:15 "I am with you and will watch over you wherever you go, and I will bring you back to this land. I will not leave you until I have done what I have promised you."

On November 22nd 2007 at 10.49 am, my baby daughter was born weighing in at 6lbs. 12 ozs. Dwane, my mother in law and Brittany were there to witness the miracle of a tiny human being opening her eyes to the world. The actuality of me being pregnant at that time and giving birth to a healthy baby girl still to this day amazes me. She was and is the perfect gift from God.

The following January provided me an opportunity to speak once more at the Right to Life weekend at Grace Church. I had come full circle. I had committed the act of abortion on that sanctified weekend; I had given my testimony five years later and I was now publicly giving my thanks to the Lord on Right to Life weekend by having my daughter Dedicated to Him. What a journey I had been on and one that I vowed I would commit my life to in helping to stop the death of babies that are given to the world as a precious gift for our future.

Ten years on and as I write this Gwen is now almost three. I hope through this account she can be a light of hope for the world in the battle to end abortion. My days are no longer filed with agony and despair that once so readily

Tracy Bihary

consumed every part of my being and soul. The anger and grief was replaced by understanding, love and above all faith in my Lord who saved my baby and who saved me.

To any mother who is considering aborting her baby; know that the Lord is with you and has given this baby to you as a gift. He is always with us, yet sadly I didn't realize that on the day that I laid down on that table in that cold dark room. He was there waiting to take my baby into His arms and I believe he cried a tear for me as he smiled into my little one's eyes. He knew the battle that lay ahead for me but also knew that the inner fight would continue to stop the endless deaths carried out each year.

Speak with Him and ask him to help you for He will be there every step of the way. Stop and think before you take action to give your baby back to the Lord. Don't live the life I lived. Enjoy your precious baby with all the love you have. Pray for the children and pray for the mothers. There are other options rather than the finality of abortion.

To my family and friends, I thank you for your endless love and faith; help me on this plight and help the world to see that one life saved is a life to be lived to the glory of God. Children are indeed a gift of the Lord; a gift that is so often thrown away without care or thought.

Savannah Grace; you are the inspiration to me every day working towards ending abortion not only in this country but the world. I love you.

8601524R0

Made in the USA
Lexington, KY
14 February 2011